MENTOR RELATIONSHIPS

How They Aid Creative Achievement, Endure, Change, and Die

E. PAUL TORRANCE

Contents

This book is dedicated
to the young adults
who shared their experiences
about their mentors.

Foreword

It seems appropriate that a book on Mentoring would be produced by E. Paul Torrance, a man who has served as a mentor to countless persons during his long and illustrious career as an educator. As I reflect on what he has meant to me personally, beginning with my graduate school days more than a decade ago, I keep returning to the thought that my life is vastly richer for having known him. I know that others who entered this relationship with him share this feeling.

Such influence of one individual on the lives of others is not unique to modern times. As Torrance notes, this sort of relationship has occurred throughout history and its importance has been alluded to over and over. The significant questions are *why* and *how* the relationship produces such positive benefits in terms of personal growth. This book addresses these questions in an analytical, yet imaginative manner.

Excellent documentation from Torrance's 22-year study of adult creative achievement is provided to describe how the relationship develops, grows and changes. Numerous anecdotes, coupled with vivid quotations from mentees, allow a thorough analysis of the kinds of encouragement and support the mentor supplies for building self-confidence, developing thinking skills and nurturing creative growth. Moreover, in his characteristic manner of original thinking, Torrance provides the "unusual twist" by analyzing what damages may occur when a person is mentorless.

Finally, I would like to note that publication of this book may also be appropriate from a societal historical standpoint. Because of our increasing population and changing work patterns, children are spending increased time with their peers and reduced time with adults. Given this trend, it seems important that we attempt to develop methods of providing opportunities for young people to spend more time with adults, particularly on a one-to-one level. The success of various Big/Brother—Big/Sister-type programs speaks to the need for children to spend time with adults.

Attempting to provide organizational support for this need, many schools and other public agencies are establishing programs designed to lead to the mentor-mentee relationship. We established a career education program at Texas A&M University in 1977, in which local high school students spend two hours a day for several months with university professors as observer/aides who are called "Mentors." In many cases, a true relationship developed and it has been very gratifying over the years to see the benefit to the students. Torrance's book would certainly provide insightful reading for anyone attempting to establish such a program.

William R. Nash, *Director*
Gifted & Talented Institute
Texas A&M University

Preface

I am indebted to many of my associates for their assistance and inspiration in preparing this publication. Dr. Felice Kaufmann designed the questions on mentors and collected similar data on the Presidential Scholars. Dr. Marilyn Rieger assisted in the collection of the data, as did Ms. Berenice Bleedorn and Ms. Rose Schaffhausen. Mr. Tzuhui Wu performed the statistical analyses of the data. Ms. Peggy Hooper and Ms. Deborah Weiner made many suggestions and stimulated me by their interest. The study participants, their elementary school teachers, and many of the parents of the program participants deserve an enormous amount of gratitude.

Those who have cast me in the role of mentor have taught me much and facilitated my survival beyond what I can say. My own most important mentor, Pansy Nigh Torrance, was always there with her love, suggestions, and help.

E. P. Torrance

CHAPTER ONE

Do Mentors Really Aid Creative Achievement?

For centuries it has been said that almost always, wherever independence and creativity occur and persist and important creative achievements occur, there is some other person who plays the role of mentor, sponsor, patron, or guru. Until the past few years, such assertions remained unchallenged and few people paid attention to them. Little effort was made to take advantage of this insight and translate it into educational programs or management practices. Nevertheless, some people continued to be and/or have mentors, sponsors, patrons, or gurus, and in recent years, educational institutions, businesses, and industrial organizations have started formal mentoring programs.

When mentoring programs started becoming more popular, old assertions and assumptions about the value of a mentor were challenged. Do mentors really make a difference? Are mentors really helpful to the creatively gifted person? Are they a "blessing" or a "curse"? For example, H. B. Crandall (1981) surveyed various viewpoints in the controversy over the value of a mentor in fostering a successful career. He solicited opinions on such statements as:

It is hard to get along without a mentor . . .
Mentors are a highly overrated factor . . .
It doesn't hurt to have one . . .
Having one can hurt your career . . .
All of the above.

After his review of many persons' careers, Crandall concluded that "all of the above" is an appropriate response. In this monograph, data from my longitudinal study (Torrance, 1981) will be used to help answer such questions as:

Do mentors really make a difference in creative achievement?
Who are mentors and what do they actually do?
Are mentor relationships always temporary and short-term?
How do mentor relationships change?
What causes mentor relationships to "sour" and be terminated?
How can mentorship programs in schools and business be strengthened?

THE MENTORSHIP CONCEPT

The term "mentor" seems to have originated from Homer's epic, *the Odyssey*. Before Ulysses embarked on his long adventure, he chose his wise and trusted friend Mentor to guard, guide, and teach his son, Telemachus. Those who have guarded, guided, and taught young persons in such relationships have borne varying labels in other cultures and periods of history with only slightly different meanings. Thus, we have had "sponsors," "patrons," "gurus," "senseis," and others. Now, the term "mentor" seems to be generally approved, at least in the United States.

In *Guiding Creative Talent*, I (Torrance, 1962) pointed out that numerous researchers observed that generally wherever independence and creativity flourished, there has been some kind of "sponsor" or "patron." I explained that this role is filled by a nonmember of the mentee's peer group who possesses prestige and power in the same social system. The mentor does several things. He/she encourages and supports the other in expressing and testing his ideas and in thinking through things. He/she protects (guards) the individual against reaction from peers and superiors long enough for the person to test and modify his/her ideas. He/she can keep the situation open enough for originality to occur and persist.

The concept of a "mentor" includes all of this and more. Noller (1982) concluded that the present interpretation of "mentor" includes more than might be implied by the definition in Webster's Second Unabridged Dictionary (i.e., a wise and faithful counselor, prudent advisor, or monitor and, loosely, a teacher or instructor). In my longitudinal study, as well as in Kaufmann's (1979) examination of President Scholars, "mentor" was defined as "an older person in your occupational field or educational experience who 'took you under his/her wing.'" In these descriptions, the mentor relationship is characterized by depth and caring.

Typically, discussions about the importance of mentoring in creative achievement have been based upon analyses of biographies and autobiographies of high-achieving, notable creative people [e.g., Goertzel & Goertzel, 1962; Goertzel, Goertzel & Goertzel, 1978); intensive case studies such as Daniel Levinson's (1978) examination of Yale University students; or as a part of psychometric studies of eminent scientists such as Anne Roe's (1953) work in the 1940s and 1950s]. Previous studies, however, have not used the presence of a mentor as a statistical predictor of creative achievement and have not tried to empirically study the characteristics, functions, development, termination, and persistence of mentor relationships.

GENERAL OVERVIEW OF THE LARGER STUDY

While this publication deals only with the role of mentors in creative achievement, the data used as its basis is a part of a much larger longitudinal study (Torrance, 1980, 1981, 1982, 1982; Torrance & Wu, 1981) and a general overview seems desirable.

From 1958 through 1964, all pupils in grades 1 through 6 in two Minnesota elementary schools were given various batteries of the *Torrance Tests of Creative Thinking* (Torrance, 1962, 1966, 1974) each year. In 1979-80, followup data of adolescent and adult creative behavior were obtained from 220 (118 women and 102 men) of the 400 originally tested for three or more years. However, complete data for the present study were available for only 212 subjects (96 men and 116 women).

Four indexes of adult creative achievement were derived from questionnaire responses: (1) number of publicly-recognized and acknowledged post-high school creative achievements; (2) number of post-high school "creative style of life achievements" not publicly recognized; (3) ratings of the quality of the highest creative achievements described; and (4) ratings of the creative quality of aspirations and future career images described. Copies of the Creative Achievement Questionnaire and the Creative Style of Life Achievement Questionnaire used in deriving the four indexes of creative achievement will be found on pages 58-62.

Pearson product moment coefficients of correlation between the Creativity Index (a composite of scores from three consecutive years of creativity testing) and each of the adult creative achievement criteria are significant at better than the .001 level, ranging from .46 for number of publicly-recognized creative achievements to .58 for rated quality of highest creative achievements. A multiple correlation coefficient of .62 was obtained through stepwise regression. While these predictive validity coefficients leave considerable variance in adult creative achievements unexplained, I believe they are about as high as we can reasonably expect. Obviously, teachers, motivation, skills, and opportunities make a difference, as do numerous other factors such as the quality of an individual's living environment.

There are, of course, many other aspects of the larger study. However, this overview should provide an adequate sketch of the present study.

THE MENTOR STUDY

In the 22-year longitudinal study, these questions were asked about the subjects' mentor experiences:

1. Have you ever had a mentor—an older person in your occupational field or educational experience who "took you under his/her wing?"
2. If you had more than one mentor, please select the one that influenced you most. Was this person male or female?
3. What was this person's official position?
4. How long was this person your mentor?
5. Approximately how much older than you was this person?
6. What did this person do that influenced you the most?
7. If you no longer consider this person your mentor, what were the circumstances of the termination of the mentorship?
8. How do you feel about this person now? Why do you feel this way?
9. Have you adopted any qualities of this person as your own?
10. If yes, please specify. If no, please discuss why you chose not to adopt any of his/her qualities.

In addition, the mentor study also made use of data about educational experiences, reports of spurs and obstacles to achievement, descriptions of frustrations and ratings of satisfaction in twelve aspects of life (work, recognition, challenge, income, marital status, children, leisure activities, friendships, community involvement, opportunity for independent action, creative output, and joy in living), and statements about dreams or hopes for the future.

DOES HAVING A MENTOR MAKE A DIFFERENCE IN CREATIVE ACHIEVEMENT?

Using the four measures of creative achievement previously described, correlation coefficients were computed for having or not having a mentor (biserial correlation). The results are shown in Table 1 separately for males, females, and the number of study participants. The table shows that only one correlation measure fails to reach significance at the five percent level (number of creative style of life or unrecognized

TABLE 1

Having a Mentor as a Predictor of Adult Creative Achievement

Criterion of Creative Achievement	r		
	Males (N = 96)	Females (N = 116)	Total (N = 212)
Rated Quality of Adult Creative Achievement	.33***	.33***	.34***
Rated Creativeness of Future Career Image	.20*	.27**	.24***
Number of Recognized Creative Achievements	.28**	.21*	.24***
Number of Creative Style of Life Achievements	.18	.24*	.22**

$* \, p < .05$ $** \, p < .01$ $*** \, p < .001$

achievements for males). The closest set of relationships is for the index obtained from the rated quality of highest adult creative achievements described by the participants.

Thus, the presence or absence of a mentor makes a difference that cannot be explained by chance.

DOES HAVING A MENTOR MAKE A DIFFERENCE IN AMOUNT OF EDUCATION COMPLETED?

Many of the participants in the study entered college and were disappointed to find that the available programs did not meet their needs and dropped out. Frequently, mentors seem to be able to help such disillusioned students either find alternative programs or to develop a satisfactory program within the existing framework. Thus we asked, "Does having a mentor make a difference in the amount of education the mentee completes?"

An index of the number of years completed by each subject was compiled. In addition to traditional college and university achievements, time spent in trade or technical schools, special schools in the arts, and post-doctoral studies was counted. The resulting means, standard deviations, and tests of significance of differences are shown in Table 2.

TABLE 2
Means and Standard Deviations for Amount of Education Completed by Subjects With and Without Mentors and Tests of Significance of Differences in Means

Sex and Mentor-ship Category	Years of Education				Level of Significance
	Number	Mean	St. Dev.	F-ratio	
Men, No Mentor	56	15.8	2.6		
Men, Mentor	40	17.8	2.4	15.36	.0002
Women, No Mentor	59	14.9	2.1		
Women, Mentor	57	18.1	2.3	59.33	.0001

The evidence in the table is clear. Mentors do make a difference for both men and women. All groups attained relatively high levels of education, the lowest being women with no mentors and the highest being females with mentors.

A possible limitation of these findings might be mentioned. Some might argue that the more education people acquire, the better the chances of finding mentors. However, only about one-third of the mentors were associated with college, university, or professional school experiences.

CONCLUSION

Despite such limitations as possible geographical, historical, socioeconomic, and other biases, the evidence in Tables 1 and 2 deserves serious consideration. At least, it has been demonstrated empirically that mentors can make a difference in the creative achievements and educational attainments of mentees.

CHAPTER TWO

Who Are Mentors And What Do They Do?

WHAT ABOUT SEX AND MENTORING?

It is not surprising that 73 percent of the mentors described by subjects in the longitudinal study are men. Historically, most mentors have been men (Halcomb, 1980), partly because there are more men in positions to assume mentor roles. As more women have moved into executive positions and other leadership roles, they are available to become mentors (*Business Week,* October 23, 1978).

What may be surprising, however, is that a slightly higher percentage of the women in this study had mentors than men. Forty-nine percent of the women and 42 percent of the men claimed to have had a mentor. Historically, mentoring relationships have not been as available to women as to men (Cook, 1979). However, there has been some tendency to use mentorships as a part of effective equal opportunity programs (Rowe, 1981). This trend may have benefited some women in this study, since they entered the employment field through the benefit of equal opportunity programs. Although the difference in percentages of males and females having mentors in this study is a chance difference, this finding is noteworthy in light of historical perspectives.

There has been discussion (Halcomb, 1980; Quinn, 1980) of the desirability of same-sex mentors. A major argument is that same-sex mentors can serve as role models as well as effective mentors. About the only difference was the greater dominance of women with male mentors when compared with women having female mentors. However, women with male mentors reported a greater need for a more personal or friendship relationship than did their counterparts with female mentors.

Table 3 presents the distributions of male and female mentors described by male and female subjects. As might be expected, few males had female mentors while over half the females had male mentors. The observed differences in proportions are statistically significant. Nevertheless, the fact that 42 percent of the women had female mentors probably reflects a greater availability of female mentors, at least from an historical perspective.

TABLE 3
Comparison of Males and Females on Sex of Mentor

Sex of Mentor	Sex of Subject					
	Males		Females		Males & Females	
	Number	Percent	Number	Percent	Number	Percent
Males	38	95	33	58	71	73
Females	2	5	24	42	26	27

Chi Square = 16.49; $p < .001$

WHAT ARE THE OFFICIAL POSITIONS OF MENTORS?

There has been discussion (Noller & Frey, 1983) about the official position of a desirable mentor. However, there seems to be little research information even about the official positions and/or relationships of mentors and their mentees.

Data regarding the official positions reported for mentors in my longitudinal study are presented in Table 4 separately for males, females, and males and females combined. For the entire group, the most frequently reported mentor position was that of a person with expertise in the mentee's field of interest. Almost as frequently mentioned was the position of professor or other post-secondary school teacher. Another frequently-mentioned group was on-the-job colleagues—employers, supervisors, and co-workers. Only nine percent of the mentors were elementary or secondary school teachers or counselors. Only two peers and two parents were mentioned as mentors. However, some subjects with mentors in other categories mentioned that their parents or their fathers had been their most important mentors. In some cases where no mentor was claimed, it was clear from other information in the questionnaire that one or both parents filled strong mentor roles.

There was a slight tendency for mentors of the males to originate in the workplace and for those of the females to be drawn from the mentee's occupation outside the workplace.

WHAT FUNCTIONS DO MENTORS PERFORM?

In mentoring literature, the relationship is generally seen as a deeper and more caring one than coach and sponsor relationships (Atkinson,

TABLE 4
Comparison of Males and Females on Position of Mentors

Position of Mentor	Males Number	Percent	Females Number	Percent	Combined Number	Percent
Elementary/high school teacher/ counselor	4	10	5	9	9	9
Professor, post-secondary teacher	12	30	19	33	31	32
Experienced person in occupation	11	27.5	22	39	33	34
Employer/super-visor/co-worker	11	27.5	9	16	20	21
Peer/parent	2	5	2	3	4	4

Chi Square = 2.66;　not significant

Alberts, Belcher, Bellman, Grote, Hayes, Laird, Mahoney & Mirabel, 1980). Some writers highlight the fact that mentors open new careers and hobby vistas (Bridges, 1980). Others feature the possibility that mentors help promising young people learn to take risks and to work with people in an intuitive and empathetic way (Collins & Scott, 1978). Still others (Fitt & Newton, 1918) see an important function of mentors as assuring mentees of getting credit for their achievements.

Data regarding the functions reported for mentors in this study are shown in Table 5. In interpreting these data, it should be noted that a single mentor might perform more than one function listed in the table. Thus, tests of the chance occurrence of differences between men and women were computed for each of the five functions.

For the group, the function most frequently described as important is encouraging, praising, and prodding. This was mentioned more frequently by women than by men (chi square = 3.55, significant at the 5 percent level). The males more frequently mentioned the importance of getting career, business, or professional information from their mentors than the females (55 percent for males and 12 percent for females; chi square = 20.47, significant at the .001 level). It is also interesting to note that 42 percent of the mentors were seen as provid-

TABLE 5
Comparison of Males and Females on functions Performed by Mentors

Function Performed by Mentor	Males No.	Males Pct.	Females No.	Females Pct.	Combined No.	Combined Pct.	Chi Square
Taught how to play the "game"	9	23	11	19	20	21	0.15
Helped make career choice	2	5	2	4	4	4	0.13
Encouraged, praised, prodded	14	35	31	54	45	46	3.55*
Career, business, professional information	22	55	7	12	29	30	20.47**
Model of behavior	14	35	27	47	41	42	1.47

* Significant at about .05 level
** Significant at better than .001 level

ing role models for their proteges. Twenty-one percent also saw their mentors as teaching them how "to play the game."

DO MENTEES ADOPT CHARACTERISTICS OF THEIR MENTORS?

A few writers (Blackburn, Chapman & Cameron, 1981) have been concerned about the possible "cloning" effect of the mentor relationship. In the academic situation, evidence seems to indicate the possibility of a significant relationship between the productivity and success of mentees and their mentors. In my longitudinal study, subjects were asked whether they adopted any characteristics of their mentors and to indicate which ones, if any, they accepted and avoided, and why. The results are summarized in Table 6. In the group, 84 percent of the subjects having mentors said they had adopted some of their mentor's characteristics. The proportions for males and females are almost identical. This suggests that even opposite-sex mentors may serve as role models, at least to some extent.

TABLE 6
Comparison of Males and Females on Adoption of Characteristics of
Mentor

Adoption Category	Males		Females		Combined	
	Number	Percent	Number	Percent	Number	Percent
Adopted Some	34	85	47	82	81	84
Adopted None	6	15	10	18	16	16

Chi Square = 0.11; not significant

TABLE 7
Positive Characteristics of Mentors Mentioned Most Frequently by
Males and Females Responding to Followup Questionnaire

Females (N = 57)		Males (N = 40)	
Characteristic Described	Percent Cited	Characteristic Described	Percent Cited
Encouraging, praising	45.6	Skilled, expert	62.5
Skilled, expert	29.8	A friend	27.5
A friend	15.8	Encouraging, prodding	25.0
Inspiring, energizing	14.0	Respectful	17.5
Supportive	14.0	Guiding	15.0
Acknowledged talent	12.3	Caring, interested	12.5
Confidence giving	12.3	Motivating	12.5
Caring, interested	12.3	Committed, dedicated	12.5
Persistent	8.8	Hard working	12.5
		Honesty	12.5

WHAT CHARACTERISTICS OF MENTORS
ARE MOST VALUED?

On the basis of the subjects' responses to the questions about how their mentors had influenced them and what mentor characteristics they adopted, a tabulation was made of the most highly-prized mentor characteristics. The results are shown in Table 7 for the ten characteristics most frequently mentioned by both males and females. Although there are similarities in the lists, indications are that the mentor needs of males and females differ in some ways.

The males more frequently prize their mentor's skill and expertise (62.5 percent compared with 29.8 percent) and the females more frequently prize encouragement and praise (45.6 percent compared with 25 percent). It is also interesting to note that the males tended to use the terminology "encourage and prod" while the females usually used the terms "encourage and praise." Friendship seems to be valued about equally by both sexes, with males mentioning it somewhat more frequently, usually in connection with continuing aspects of the mentor relationship.

Some other terms capturing special mentor needs of the males include: active, challenging, committed and dedicated, controversial, courageous, guiding, hardworking, involved, love of his/her work, motivated for excellence, problem solving, receptive, and stern.

Characteristics that seem to capture mentor needs of the women include: ability to acknowledge the talents of others, articulateness, calmness, consideration of alternatives, confidence giving, controlled, empathetic, enthusiastic, facilitative, even-tempered, humble, idealistic, patient, non-violent philosophy, relaxed, thorough, vital, and witty.

Characteristics that seemed to alienate women included: ambitiousness, compulsivity to work, critical in judgment, dominating and intimidating manner, lack of empathy, lack of future orientation, high standards, hypocrisy, intolerance of the ideas of others, inflexibility, perfectionism, and trendiness.

CHAPTER THREE

Are Mentor Relationships Temporary?

Generally, the mentor relationship has been regarded as a temporary, transitory one (Levinson, 1978). Most current programs in gifted education, career counseling, and professional training have been set up for brief periods—two weeks, six weeks, six months. A summer mentorship program in Minnesota (Mansergh, Jeska-Silrum, Ames & Hansen, 1982) for junior and senior high school students was conducted for six weeks. A career education program established at Texas A & M University for senior high school students (Colson, 1980) operated on a nine-month basis but the mentorship and internship phases lasted for only six months. An alumni group at the University of Minnesota School of Journalism and Mass Communication (1983) operated on a ten-week basis. Perhaps since the mentorship relationship has been regarded as temporary and transitory and recently developed programs have operated with short time-spans, little scientifically developed information exists about the way mentorship relationships develop, endure, die, or change over time. In my longitudinal study, I (Torrance, 1980, 1981, 1982) have developed some information providing immediate guidance and preparing the way for more intensive studies.

HOW DO YOUNG ADULTS FEEL ABOUT THEIR MENTORS NOW?

There is a popular belief that mature adults ultimately feel negative about their mentors. Their mentors may have been unable to live up to the mentees' high expectations of them. Mentees may come to feel they had been exploited by their mentors. Mentors may have tried to impose intolerable expectations on them. Or, the mentors may have revealed imperfections. This has happened to many of our national heroes. Benjamin Franklin was a womanizer. Thomas Jefferson fathered illegitimate black children, and Albert Einstein was suspected of being involved in all kinds of communist plots.

Data concerning the present feelings of participants in this study about their mentors are presented in Table 8. Seventy-three percent of those studied expressed "very positive" feelings about their mentors and 87 percent expressed "positive" or "very positive" feelings about them.

TABLE 8
Comparison of Males and Females on Present Feelings About Mentors

Feeling Category	Males		Females		Combined	
	Number	Percent	Number	Percent	Number	Percent
Negative	0	0	3	5	3	3
Ambivalent/ neutral	3	7.5	7	12	10	10
Positive	2	5	11	19	13	14
Very positive	35	87.5	36	63	71	73

Chi Square = 8.11; $p < .05$

There is a general tendency for women to express more dissatisfaction with their mentors than men. This is not a chance difference (chi square = 8.11, significant at better than the 5 percent level of confidence). Without examining the source data, one might speculate that this difference is because many of the women had opposite-sex mentors while few men had women as mentors. A closer look at the data indicates, however, that most mentors drawing negative or ambivalent feelings from their female proteges were women.

ARE MENTOR RELATIONSHIPS ALWAYS TEMPORARY?

Despite the fact that the mentor relationship has been regarded as temporary, 52 percent of the subjects with mentors reported that this relationship has persisted. Forty-five percent of the men and 56 percent of the women reported such continuing relationships. Some of these relationships have changed from a mentor relationship to another form, to be explained below. The mean duration of the mentor relationship at the time of the follow-up was 4.2 years.

DOES THE INFLUENCE OF EARLY MENTORS PERSIST?

Only nine percent of the study participants named an elementary or high school teacher, counselor, or administrator as their most important or influential mentor. However, it was clear from other information on follow-up questionnaires that many others experienced such relationships and that such mentoring continues to play a role in the creative successes of these young adults.

The following statement by one of the most creative males in the study attests to this continuing influence:

> My most important mentor was my fourth-grade teacher. In many ways he provided an impetus to synthesize in what is, I am told, my radical brain. Fourth grade ended but his influence has been permanent. I have not heard from him in 11 years, but I am still grateful. I hope that I have continued to synthesize aspects of the sciences, arts, and humanities, which was, in great part what—school was all about.

This young man at age 30 today is still doing many of the things that his fourth-grade teacher/mentor encouraged and gave him a chance to do.

This former teacher has continued to be a mentor for several study participants and I know personally of two young men he "mentored" through stressful young adult crises. Recently, he sent me a letter he received from one of his former students, who is now a lawyer. He reported on a recent trip he made to visit several of his elementary school classmates who were subjects of this study. He closed his letter with the following remarks:

> . . . and now that I am home, I have suppressed one of my occasional longings for simpler times by writing to you . . . Over the years I have spent so much time talking about grade school that _____ (his wife) is anxious to meet you and your family.

A highly creative woman in the study made this comment about the influence of her elementary school mentors:

> I am particularly pleased to be basically following through on a talent nurtured way back in the _____Elementary School—further directed in college and nine years later after college I am still making it. I don't know the dropout rate in other fields, but practicing artists, after leaving the academic environment and working to support themselves in the "real world" find it very hard to keep up the output. I have been fortunate . . .

Since the basic question in the follow-up questionnaire about mentors established a mental set for mentoring at the young adult stage and asked for information about only one mentor, it is not surprising that only nine respondents named elementary and high school mentors as most important. This is a defect in the present study and should be remedied in future studies. The follow-up data, however, provides considerable information about the need for mentors at an early age and missed opportunities for effective mentoring. Highly gifted and/or creative disadvantaged children especially need mentors to help them pursue something they are "in love with" and might become a highly successful creative career.

DO PARENTS SERVE AS MENTORS?

Daniel Levinson (1978) and his associates concluded that a mentor is a mixture of parent and peer. Thus, it is not surprising that many study participants mentioned mentoring behavior by their parents, especially their fathers. Only three, however, named their fathers as their most important mentor. Several others mentioned that their parents had had more influence on the development of their personal characteristics and their learning "to play the game" than had their mentors. Some also named a non-parent as their most important mentor in response to the mentor question but indicated elsewhere that their real mentor had been a parent.

One of the creative young women in the study called her father her most important mentor and wrote:

> He taught me the value of honesty. He is my friend. He listens to me as I do to him. I value his judgment and we help each other in our work. He encourages me to try whatever I would like. He never condemns me or berates me and knows that I would help him in any way I can.

About adopting his characteristics, she stated:

> I have his nose for one thing! Also arthritis. I have his passion for hard work, organic mindedness, and non-violent philosophy.

DOES A YOUNG PERSON MISS ANYTHING
BY NOT HAVING A MENTOR AT AN EARLY AGE?

Many highly creative study participants suffered a great deal and were retarded in their development by delays in getting a mentor. One young woman with a successful career in theater and dance made this observation about not having a mentor during her early years:

> I didn't begin to live, to enjoy myself or have faith in my

abilities until college. I never worked consistently until age 17. The past 11 years have been like the first 11 years of my life. I am only beginning to find out about myself rather late in life . . .

Another young woman, with a successful creative writing career, described some of her pains resulting from the lack of an early mentor:

> I am a writer today, but not until college did I realize that I had any unusual ability. My elementary school experiences were awful. I got perfect marks for organization, spelling, and punctuation, but was graded down for having lousy handwriting. I also was never told that anything I did was original . . . I always wanted to be a writer but didn't know if I could be . . . I wanted to be creative, but I was terrible in art, so I thought I was a dud. I also never wrote about what I really thought about for teachers, because they wouldn't understand.
>
> If someone had told me back then that I was creative, I would have had something to hold on to. All I knew was that I was different. I had a very unhappy childhood and adolescence, but a pretty satisfying life as an adult. It would have been nice to have been encouraged when I was younger. Continue your work. Kids like I was need someone to help.

As Toynbee (1964), the eminent historian, pointed out, ability in a child can be discouraged easily. Children are quite vulnerable to discouragement. They are even more sensitive to hostile public opinion than adults, and as Toynbee maintains, they "are even readier to purchase, at almost any price, the toleration that is an egalitarian society's alluring reward for poor spirited conformity." Some children's struggle to maintain creativity is a losing one, especially among poverty-stricken youth. Many surrender their creativity by the end of third grade and never regain it (Torrance, 1962, 1965).

One young woman in this study offers a heart-rending example of this phenomenon. When she was in the first grade, she had an estimated IQ of 177 and had the highest creativity score of any first grader in the study. Her first-grade teacher and her parents were disturbed that this six-year-old still had imaginary playmates. The teacher, parents, and the school social worker all tried to help this girl rid herself of imaginary playmates, failing almost completely to acknowledge her multi-giftedness. By the end of the third grade, her IQ was 110 and her creativity scores were below average for her grade level. She dropped out of school in the tenth grade to help care for her family. She was married at age 19 and had three boys in rapid order. This comment was on her follow-up questionnaire:

> Someday I would like to finish high school and maybe go into nursing, something that really interests me. But I don't think I am very smart. There is lots in life to learn.

This highly gifted first grader came from an economically deprived home and lived in what the teachers referred to as "the project." One wonders what might have happened had the school helped find her a mentor rather than sending a social worker to dispose of her imaginary playmates.

WHAT ARE SOME PROBLEMS OF SUSTAINING MENTOR RELATIONSHIPS?

While the mentor relationship is generally regarded as a transitional one in the early part of a person's career, many subjects expressed a need for a sustained mentor relationship and for finding new mentors as career changes were made. In the future, this may become a more important consideration, if it is true that most people change careers several times during their lifetime.

One creative young woman who terminated a mentor relationship with her dissertation advisor still "harbors considerable feelings of anger" and this appears to inhibit her in seeking or accepting another mentor now that she faces a career change. She writes about her present conflict:

> I find myself at a choice point and feel uncomfortably pulled in several directions. Forego a nationally respected research career or develop excellence as a psychotherapist-clinician or delegate employment interests to a smaller role titled "job" and put energy into an as yet undefined area. The result is a lack of confidence in my skills and talents and a general lack of enthusiasm. I have no real creative outlet presently (other than challenge of diagnostic puzzles presented by clients) and look forward to returning to dance or painting, or something else to fill the void.

Several subjects recognized that although their mentors helped them early in their career, they had outgrown their mentors. They seemed to have difficulties, however, in replacing their castoff mentors. These comments by a woman in the visual arts field are illustrative:

> I became disillusioned with his painting and his criticisms of mine, feeling that both were too limited. I feel that he helped me a lot for a while but that I've gotten all I can from him. He is too limited. He doesn't see far enough beyond the styles of the moment . . . I have intermittent difficulty with my work; more specifically, a sort of blockage that sometimes happens which makes it hard to paint with the intensity I desire . . .

From the subjects' data, it is difficult to surmise what sustains a mentorship and results in mutual satisfaction. It seems certain that both persons in a mentorship must continue to grow and contribute to each other's growth. In the following description of a sustained mentorship involving a creative young woman, it seems to be the integrity of the mentor and the diplomatic skills of the mentee:

> He is still my mentor, although he has not always been the only mentor in my life. I trust him completely for in eight years he has never given me cause to feel otherwise. This is unusual, for I fear I tend to distrust most people . . . I have tried to be as committed to excellence in work as he is . . . If one can label it creative, my greatest skill is bringing different people to a consensus. I'm recognized as a "diplomat," "negotiator," or "arbitrator."

The Governor of her state appointed her to an important commission to develop alternative correctional programs/procedures to imprisonment.

WHAT HAPENS WHEN MENTORS LACK POWER TO INTERVENE SUCCESSFULLY FOR THEIR MENTEES?

Although mentors, like patrons or sponsors, usually have some power and are able to help their proteges secure the opportunities they merit and desire, sometimes they are unsuccessful. Such was the case of one of the most creative males in the study. He wanted a career in medicine, won many scholastic and leadership honors along the way, and appeared headed for a successful medical career. However, he was eliminated by the objective examination required by the system. In this case a subject's superior divergent thinking abilities led him to achievements that conflicted with the rigid requirements and "the right answers" honored by the established system. From an independent source, I understand he was able to impress the examiners by his explanations for his incorrect responses on the examination. While the examiner admitted that the student's insights were keener than those of most students who passed the examination, he did not have the power to give his mentee a chance to study medicine, even though he was an associate dean in the medical school. However, the mentee maintained a positive attitude, as indicated:

> My mentor gave support through rough times and added perspective in good times. When I left school, he no longer made efforts to keep in contact. I have missed the close contact with him. He was a great part of my life.

Unrealistic expectations about the power of mentors seems to be especially prevalent in business. Louise Kelley (1982) has cautioned young women about the dangers of expecting too much from the power of mentors to help them find successful corporate careers. She had been told that having a mentor was the key to success in a business situation. She had been warned about the risk of a "painful passage" when the mentorship relationship might end suddenly because of the mentor's feeling of rejection and the mentee's needs for independence. She discovered that mentors can be harmful to health and career, and believes that having a male mentor can be especially damaging to a woman's reputation. She also asserts that male mentors are unable to understand a younger female manager. Such a woman also becomes the object of organizational mistrust. Furthermore, there is a tendency for a female mentee with a male mentor to become overdependent and fail to develop personally and professionally.

CHAPTER FOUR

How Do Mentor
Relationships Change?

In the preceding chapter, it is apparent that many mentor relationships endure. This is to be expected. If that is the case, it may be expected that the relationship will change with time as both mentor and
mentee grow. If either fails to grow, the relationship is likely to turn
sour and ultimately die. In this chapter, I shall use data from the longitudinal study to examine how the mentoring relationship changes
with time.

WHAT ARE THE MOST FREQUENT KINDS OF CHANGE?

The two most frequently reported changes in direction of the mentoring relationship were the colleague and the friend relationships. This
statement by a highly creative man describes a relationship that
seems to reflect both of these directions:

> We have developed a close relationship, a close friendship.
> As my knowledge of the field has widened, our exchanges
> have become more equitable. We also share athletic inter-
> ests and our lifestyles are also similar in many ways. I have
> adopted some of his social skills in meeting and dealing
> with people, his scientific approach, and his way of thinking
> of a problem in terms of an exactly stated question.

Here the mentor has served as a role model, a frequently recognized
phenomenon. However, as the mentee matured, the mentor and the
mentee became real colleagues, with the mentee contributing to the
knowledge and growth of the mentor. With the increased rate of
change, expansion of knowledge and the creation of new technology,
this aspect of the mentor-mentee relationship is certain to become
more crucial and frequent.

One of the creative females describes a similar transition:

> We are still good friends. She has continued to support my
> moves in the theater and to be encouraging, although our
> interests have diverged. I can still discuss our profession al-
> though several differences in opinion and attitude exist.

When differences in opinions and attitudes develop, the relationship
may become distant and even hostile. Such differences are frequently

seen as threatening by some mentors and they reject the mentee. However, as in this case, the mentor may continue to be supportive and friendship may endure.

Another creative woman in the study describes the transformation of the mentor relationship to a collegial one as follows:

> She introduced me to a new and different way of working with children which combines dance, music, dramatics and academics. I am still very much involved with her and have the opportunity to give a lecture in her place and to travel and give workshops with her.

The arrangement is quite common and usually seems to be mutually beneficial. The services of many mentors are in such demand that they cannot possibly respond to all requests for their services (workshops, lectures or performances). Yet the mentor wishes to provide the necessary services and see his/her ideas furthered. One of the best ways to do this is for accomplished mentees or students to provide the service. This gives the young person excellent opportunities to practice skills and invent new methods under the mentor's tutelage. Furthermore, new insights gained by mentees in providing these services can be shared by the mentor and developed and refined further.

Some subjects clearly were groping for an analogous relationship to describe evolution in their mentoring situation. Another creative woman described the change this way:

> I feel very warmly toward her—she is like a favorite aunt (almost). I respect her and am flattered by her respect for me. I suppose my present feelings are based on the accumulation of past experience and the development of our relationship as we both moved up career ladders. I see her rarely but think of her often.

As mentors and mentees become separated geographically, the relationship may continue to flourish through correspondence, telephone conversations, the exchange of writings and other creative products and occasional meetings. The spiritual aspects of the relationship may even be present.

DO MENTORS AND MENTEES REVERSE ROLES?

In some cases the mentor relationship evolved slowly from one of pupil to teacher and from being protected to protecting. Several statements from participants in the longitudinal study will be used to document this conclusion:

> At this point I have an ever-growing love for him, although I feel a great concern because he is now in a position that inhibits his creative abilities. He suffers periods of mild depression because he has no adequate outlet for his creative efforts in choral conducting or music composition.

Some of the young people in the study experience and express great concern and sympathy for their mentors whose contributions are not adequately recognized and rewarded. Sometimes, mentees were even instrumental in helping their mentors obtain more rewarding positions and to find work environments more favorable to their creativity.

Another creative young woman wrote of her experiences in role reversal:

> I have a different lifestyle from her and I think she has adopted some of my qualities and values since I have known her. There are times when I seem to be her teacher or mentor.

Again, this occurs fairly often. Many mentees become more successful than their mentors. Some mentors are unable to accept this and reject highly successful mentees who are no longer dependent upon them. When mentors accept and enjoy the success of their mentees, adopting some of their qualities and ideas may provide a means of mutual growth.

Still another creative young woman described her relationship with her mentor in a similar manner:

> I am very fond of her. It seems as though I am now *her* mentor. She seems to feel that it is very important that I know of (and approve of) each new breakthrough in her private and professional thought. I no longer feel any need for her approval—though her approval still feels good.

In this case, the mentor now seems to be more dependent for growth upon the mentee than vice-versa. Although the mentee no longer feels a need for approval from her mentor, she still finds "it feels good" to have it. In some cultures, the mentee or pupil must sustain a mentor in his old age or failing years. For example, in Japan (Morsbach, 1978), the relationship is seen as an enduring one. The mentor (sensei) has little fear of finally being upstaged. With increasing age, the mentor can expect increased prestige through the number and accomplishments of his mentees. Mentees feel honor bound to see that their mentors get the official credit, even if it is common knowledge that this is no longer the real situation. This custom is signified by such Japanese proverbs as, "The invisible pillar holds up the house."

The following statement by a creative young man in the study reflects a cultural tradition quite different from the Japanese one described above:

> Even though his name is not a household word, he continues to persevere. He deserves much more recognition as a composer, for he is one of the giants and pioneers—innovators in his special field. I admire his conviction in himself and his continued creative output regardless of the lack of public recognition. There are times when I wish I could tell him how to get more recognition and communicate his work more widely.

It is understandable and regrettable that this young man is reluctant, perhaps with reason, to share his expertise for the benefit of his mentor, whom he admires greatly. However, if he were to offer such advice or assistance, it might be rejected. This dilemma might have been avoided if there had been greater communication of feelings in the early stages of the relationship—or if he were living in the Japanese tradition.

DO MENTORS AND MENTEES COMPETE WITH ONE ANOTHER?

Aside from the collegial and friendship relationships, the most frequent direction of the transition of the mentor relationship seems to have been to competitor. The following statement by a creative male in the study illustrates how the competitor relationship emerges and how it may be tempered with a certain kind of friendship:

> He taught me how to work hard. He taught me that anything is possible, if you work hard, have the desire and the brains—taught me something about "wheeling and dealing." I am no longer his "sidekick." I no longer put him on a pedestal, because I know he's "blue chip." He's a great guy . . . He's still my hunting partner. We have different lifestyles and don't socialize much. I am no longer his right-hand man but his competition. We kid each other a lot about the "big money" the other one makes.

Here the possible strain and threat of competition seems to be reduced by good-natured joking between mentor and mentee and occasional hunting trips. It is clear, however, that this young man genuinely respects his former mentor and it can be inferred that the mentor respects and admires his former pupil or mentee. The former mentor (now friend and competitor) probably brags to his other friends and business associates about the success of his former mentee.

A somewhat different version of the mentor to competitor relationship is described by another creative male in the study:

> He gave me more business education than any college course could have offered both educationally and politically. Thank the world for him. We still deal with one another in business and social activities. I am now a competitor of his firm.

As in the previous case, this mentee still admires and values his mentor and the relationship persists both at a social and business level. In some cases, mentors and mentees make business or professional referrals to one another. This seems to contribute to the relationship's endurance. Such arrangements are not only financially beneficial to both, but also provide a vehicle both can use to grow in business or professional expertise and recognition.

In some cases the transition of the mentor relationship to a competitive one is tainted by feelings of threat and jealousy when the mentee moves ahead of the mentor. This was described by a creative young woman in the study:

> He gave me advice about handling people. He showed me how to sell my work. He told me to be more tolerant of other people . . . I quit the firm he works for. I still see him occasionally for lunch. I feel he doesn't see that I have come a long way in the last two years. I have much better control over my insecurities. I am no longer shy when I have to sell. I make more money than he thinks I should be making at my age, which is absurd.

Some mentors are unable to see and accept the maturity, expertise and success of their mentees. Since such mentors feel their mentees are already "too successful" (making too much money or getting too much recognition), they become unwilling to continue helping them achieve even greater success.

DO MENTORS AND MENTEES FALL IN LOVE?

Since the mentor relationship is characterized by depth and caring, our society frequently suspects it has a sexual aspect. In a few instances in the study, the mentor relationship did become a love relationship. In one of the few cases in which a male had a female mentor, a young actor established a mentor relationship with a female theater director 7½ years older than himself. He describes the relationship as follows:

> She assured me of my own self-worth and provided me with a more adequate working language system by which I could speak about, criticize and hence improve my craft (a craft that deals with intangibles, ambiguities and emotions—a nonempirical craft).
>
> I fell in love with her and she with me. I still feel giddy. I am happily in love, but also have a working relationship with a colleague I respect above all others. It is the best of all possible worlds.
>
> I have not adopted any of her personal characteristics. I am not her. However, I have adopted her language system and we seem to have similar tastes and aesthetics, but I cannot ascertain if this is a product of assuming her language structure or a product of my own growing expertise.

Social and cultural pressures sometimes mitigate against the development of close mentor-mentee relationships. If the relationship becomes a close, caring one, others suspect that the mentee is being sexually exploited. There have been a number of same-sex/opposite-sex studies. Levinson (1978) found that masculine mentoring relationships were usually short and frequently ended with one or both individuals being dissatisfied with the relationship. Quinn (1980) found that the majority of the women in her study tended to continue some type of relationship with their mentors, particularly female mentors. Women with male mentors reported a greater need for a more personal or friendship aspect in the mentoring relationship than the women with female mentors.

It is apparent that some mentors deliberately set up defenses against permitting mentoring from developing into a love/sexual relationship. One senses this in the following statement by a creative young woman with a male mentor:

> I respect him. I care about his well being. However, if I were to see him again, I would make it clear that we were still

friends but not teacher to student. Circumstances before he left (he was going through a divorce and wanted a lot of distance from people) were very difficult for me and I still feel hurt from this . . .

Public suspicion as well as misunderstanding about mentoring may result from a failure to recognize the depth and caring aspects of the relationship. One of my mentees recently wrote of this matter:

> True mentorship is in a class by itself! It has nothing what-soever to do with earthly functions such as marriage, sexual love, etc. It is a spiritual and cognitive relationship where the mentor feels a responsibility to a mentee whom he knows will carry on after he is no more on this earth. It is a preparation period—preparing the mentee to go beyond where he was—time and body ran out . . . It's an extension of one's spirit. It's perpetuating and sending on to future generations what he lives and dies for, knowing that the mentee thinks and feels the same way.

CAN SPOUSES BE MENTORS?

The mentoring literature includes a few instances in which a spouse has served as a mentor. For example, Stelle Fevers (Fevers & Diamond, 1978) describes how her husband acted as her mentor, giving her en-couragement and support in insisting that she pursue her own inter-ests. With his encouragement, she found she often succeeded in doing unlikely things because she was not told they could not be done. In a few instances in my longitudinal study, spouses became mentors. This happened in the case of one highly creative woman. After an early and rather successful dancing career, she became intrigued by her hus-band's laboratory science work and became quite adept at laboratory research. She wrote about her dreams for her future career:

> In the next 10 years, I would like to have laboratory space of my own in association with my husband so that we could collaborate easily on many experiments. I would also like to see formal educational requirements become less important than actual knowledge and competence in order to help people who like to learn from our experiences.

DO MENTORS BECOME FATHER FIGURES TO MENTEES?

In some instances, the mentor relationship became one in which the mentor became a father figure. This happened to one young woman who felt her own father exploited her during her high school years and had ignored and "put down" her creativity. Here is how she described the relationship:

> I had created a way to support myself and go to college. My mentor recognized my intelligence and talents in art and guided me to pursue my interests and improve my skills. I love him. He's very much a father figure. In fact, his daughter and I are close friends. I respect his achievements in art and admire his ability to continue working, showing, managing. I appreciate his intelligence and experience. I am more down-to-earth and realize that I can't be happy with the financial insecurity of the field of art.

The "father image" some mentees have of their mentors is maintained not by the mentors' doing what the mentees' fathers do but by doing what they had wished their own fathers would. After a 14-year relationship, one contemporary of the subjects wrote her "father image" mentor as follows:

> Probably the things I appreciate most of all:
> (1) You never once made a decision for me in all these 14 years!
> (2) You gave me vital information right when I needed it.
> (3) Most of all, you continued to believe that I had worth even though I couldn't see it or feel it . . .
> (4) You have been so consistent and dependable. You were always there when I needed you most. WHERE ON EARTH DO YOU GET YOUR STRENGTH?

CHAPTER FIVE

Why Do Some Mentor Relationships Die?

The last two chapters offer many clues about the nature of the difficulties encountered in sustaining mentor relationships. Much of the data presented in these chapters, however, came from the 52% of the mentees who had sustained their relationships with mentors. In this chapter, I shall examine data supplied by the 48% who did not continue this relationship. The follow-up responses chronicle many barriers to an enduring mentor relationship. Some of the more frequently mentioned barriers will be identified and illustrated by quotations from the respondents.

THE INTIMIDATING NATURE OF THE RELATIONSHIP

In many instances mentors have considerable power over their mentees. This is especially true if the mentor is the mentee's employer, supervisor or professor. If the mentor abuses this power or if the mentor's behavior is interpreted as an abuse, trust is damaged and the relationship is likely to deteriorate and eventually die. This was expressed by one creative young woman:

> She watched me like a hawk and praised my work. She befriended me while criticizing and rejecting other newcomers. I still feel somewhat resentful. Although she helped me, I mistrusted her reasons for taking me in to the exclusion of others. She was a very intimidating person and mentorship is an intimidating relationship to outsiders.

PACE TOO FAST

In some cases, the mentor's pace is too fast or too slow for the mentee. If it is too slow, the mentee grows impatient and gradually moves away from the mentor. More frequently, however, the mentor's pace is too fast—the mentor is too ambitious or expects too much. This statement by a creative young woman illustrates how some mentees feel about this incompatibility:

> I feel respect, admiration, a little inferior to her. She paces her life faster than I feel comfortable with. I seem to have to progress at my own rate. From where I sit, her life is not

what I would like for mine to be and yet a part of me thinks I should.

MAKING SACRIFICES TO PERSONAL INTEGRITY

Several mentor relationships weakened and died when the mentee developed a growing suspicion about the sacrifices to personal integrity made by their mentors. The following statement contains one young man's expression of this distrust:

> He has an energetic approach to life, has a warm personality, and is the best engineer I have ever met. I have seen him work 18 hours a day for three months without a break. He has sacrificed a measure of personal integrity to achieve his position and retain it in a large company. I sense his desire to succeed in his work regardless of the effect on friends.

TOO LIMITED IN OUTLOOK

Several mentees drifted away from their mentors when they found the mentors were too limited in perspective and unable to look beyond present trends. In the following statement a creative young woman in the visual arts describes her experiences with such a mentor:

> He told me that I was talented, encouraged me to study painting and helped me get into a good graduate school, nominated me for honors and the like. I became disillusioned with his painting and his criticisms of mine, feeling that both of them were too limited.
>
> He helped me a lot for a while but I think I have gotten all I can from him. He is too limited. He doesn't see far enough beyond the styles of the moment. He doesn't look enough at the great art of the past.
>
> He seemed too "trendy" for me professionally, but personally there are certain characteristics of his which I find admirable and try to emulate: value placed on certain somewhat 19th Century attitudes concerning taste, wit, manners, moral principles, i.e., books vs. TV, responsibility for one's actions, etc.

SEX ROLE BARRIERS

Several young women seem to have experienced a lack of closeness in their male mentors and have searched in vain for female mentors. This statement by a very successful and creative respondent expresses the pain that caused some of these relationships to die:

A "father figure" thesis advisor whom I do not count as a real mentor. Our scholarly interests were not in agreement and I always felt at odds with him. I feel my achievements have been in spite of rather than because of "male mentor support." I never had a female teacher at Harvard or Yale, so I have never had a "role model" as such. The one tenured woman here is a superwoman—wife, mother, genius, overpowering personality, who "supports" other women, but also wants to dominate. As with men before her, I feel more at odds than sustained or encouraged . . .

RACE AS A BARRIER

Black males in the study seem to have had especially difficult times finding and maintaining mentors. One, the son of a distinguished journalist, held numerous youth leadership posts such as political aide in one presidential campaign, U.S. delegate to the World Assembly of Youth and Executive Committeeman of the U.S. Youth Council. He said he had never established a mentor relationship.

Another black male entered an elite college but dropped out because of hostile encounters with what he described as "racist instructors." He then entered a prestigous black university and quit "to find out what the world outside of academia was like." He had to withdraw a third time for financial reasons. His statement provides clues about why it is difficult for him to establish a mentor relationship with either a white or a black mentor:

I have found that I am most creative working with children and young people. I understand the world in which they live, a world that has often rejected them. I have grown as a man to see the world, society and culture in terms of black and white . . . If there is pain in my growth, it did not stem from this realization but rather the pain lies in the illusive world of gray—my standing between both the black and the white making no judgment of either . . . If I have been hurt, it has come from my friends who, after having "grown up," greet me with the statement, "I am a white person." Yes, I have grown as a man to understand that the world is full of color. One does not need to be a physicist to comprehend this fact. Even photography has transcended its black-white stage . . . However, the photographic eye is not the photographer's eye . . .

Yet the same problems appear and reappear. I guess my point is this: in how many ways does the creativity in man get stifled not because he was a child—and here I am thinking of Nietsche's "Man's tragedy is that he was a child"—but because he was black?

BEHAVIOR NOT APPROVED BY MENTOR

Many mentor relationships deteriorate and die when the mentee engages in behavior not approved by the mentor or behavior perceived by the mentee as being disapproved by the mentor. This occurs when the mentee accepts values different from the mentor's or accepts standards below the mentor's expectations. This also occurs when the mentee changes to another field and feels that he/she has "let down" the mentor. The following statement illustrates how a mentee feels when he/she has not lived up to standards once learned from the mentor:

> My mentor stimulated creativity by learning as well as by teaching. Our relationship was terminated when I got married under circumstances which were damaging to the mentor relationship. I have ambivalent feelings about him, partly because we have had no contact for several years and because of some of the qualities I admired and respected and expectations I had of myself through him have not been a part of my life . . . The qualities I respected (scholarship, integrity, honesty, open-mindedness, etc.) are not a part of my life now . . . Partly due to receiving this questionnaire at this particular time, I plan to take time off from career pursuits to explore creative potentials. I have not been true to my need to fulfill the creative surge I feel . . .

The following statement was made by one of the most intellectually brilliant women in the study, one who at the same time was relatively low on measures of creative thinking ability:

> He didn't teach me all I know but he tried very hard to teach me how "to play the game." He tried to tell me what I would need to do/be to be successful. He didn't push me at all and sometimes had trouble encouraging me but I felt he really wanted to teach and help me.

I am now somewhat afraid to face him because I have not been as successful as he hoped . . . Scientifically I feel successful, but also uncreative. My mentor's major criticism of my abilities was that he felt I didn't have or didn't pursue good ideas.

Some participants discontinued relationships with a mentor when they changed occupational fields. The following statement came from a young man whose mentor was a high school choir director. The mentee pursued a music career for several years but eventually switched fields and became quite successful in computer science.

I think we will always be friends, but when I gave up music teaching altogether, I felt that in some way I had failed him. I tried to use his teaching techniques, although I could never use his style . . .

PHILOSOPHY OF LIFE INCOMPATIBLE WITH HAVING A MENTOR

Just as some of the participants held philosophies of life mitigating against their having a mentor, some had philosophies which would preclude continuing a mentoring relationship. The following statement from a creative young man is illustrative:

I feel very strongly that people must realize and take responsibility for their lives. Most people do not and their lives are not working for them and the blame is always something exterior. I have taken responsibility for my life and it is working . . . By starting my business I can have total control over my financial state, for I am no longer working for someone else. I am also able to share my success with others who are willing to take responsibility and make efforts to change their lives for the better. I plan to be retired in the next 10 years. I dropped out of college. There was nothing I wished to gain from school so it was a waste of my time to continue. I felt that what I wished to learn I could do on my own.

WHEN CAREERS AND JOBS ARE SEPARATE

Mentor relationships seem to wither when the mentee does not earn a living in his favorite field. For example one study participant, a highly creative male, loves to fly, study, paint and create. Yet, he has been employed as a music performer, piano tuner, harpsichord builder and cabinet maker. When he completed his follow-up questionnaire, he was managing a factory producing ambulances and medical equipment. The company has 50 employees and grosses about $10 million annually. His most important mentor was a cabinet maker in a shop where he worked. His reflections about his mentor and his career follow:

> Defining career is hard. I work for Road Rescue but flying is my real career. I have a sailplane which I race around the country.
>
> My mentor showed me what professional skill (craftsmanship) is all about. I have a great deal of respect for him. He taught me a concern for the things I create. I wish I were either independently wealthy or subsidized so that I could study, paint, create and fly as I please.
>
> About six years ago when I was performing as a musician, I had an image of becoming a really top pilot. Not much later I returned to_____and began working in a factory so that I could afford to fly. I had seen sailplane flying when I was in Europe and I fell in love with the idea . . . I still have every intention of becoming a member of the U.S. Soaring Team and eventually a world champion, but my "just money job" has turned into an interesting career so I'm involved in a dual world. I have just returned from the sixth sailplane championship where I placed eighth. I'm doing well but I have a ways to go. Someday I'll be on that U.S. team.

AVERSION TO EDUCATIONAL INSTITUTIONS

Participants with mentors associated with educational institutions and who developed aversions to schools seemed unable to continue their relationships with the mentor. The following statement by a creative male illustrates this predicament:

> He chose me as a research assistant in my freshman year. I have a great deal of respect for him, but I am content to leave the relationship in the past because of my desire to stay away from educational institutions as much as possible . . . My senior independent research paper was a study on creativity, one of my primary interests.

ORIGINALITY A THREAT TO MENTORS

Many mentors become frightened of their mentees' original ideas exactly when support is needed. In the following statement, one young man in the study describes his experience:

> Most of the people with whom I have worked have felt threatened by ideas that will result in changes in the status quo. I have completed several experiments that resulted in significant process improvements. Most of the people haven't the faintest idea what I'm talking about in technical areas. I generally find support only after considerable success in ventures of limited scope.

FEELINGS OF MISTREATMENT AND HURT

Some mentor relationships die when the mentee feels the mentor has mistreated and hurt him/her. A creative young woman described her feelings this way:

> She taught me dance and used an incredible amount of drive, energy and passion to produce dances and a company that reflected what she wanted. I quit working with her in distress about the way she treated me.
>
> I have mixed feelings about her: respect for what she's accomplished and anger for how she hurt me. I am sorry that she's had to hurt so many to get where she is and I am disappointed that her current work does not excite me the way her earlier work did. I do not think that anyone has to be torn down for a person to grow and excel.

GEOGRAPHICAL DISTANCES

The most frequently offered reason for terminating the mentor relationship was geographical distance. Of course, many mentorships survive considerable separation while others continue at great distances. Nevertheless, "moving away" and the consequent separation is the single most frequently mentioned reason for the death of mentor relationships. The following are examples of this:

> . . . I moved to another part of the country. I think of him occasionally and would like to talk with him again, find out what he's doing and how he feels about it. I felt free to

develop my own style as a teacher, stick up for it and take risks to improve teaching conditions.

* *

He moved out of state and I lost contact with him. I think about him and care for him. If I were to see him again our relationship would be different.

BECOMING A HOUSEWIFE AND MOTHER

Frequently, young women's mentor relationships ended when they left their career to start a family. Two participants reflected on this:

I think my relationship with my mentor ended when I ended my active career outside my home. It is very frustrating to try to feel good about myself as a homemaker and mother in a society that does not really respect such an occupation. I also miss the stimulation of an active career outside of the home (but I do plan to return to one when the time is right).

* *

Recently I met my mentor for lunch and he seemed very distant. I suppose our relationship died when I started being a full-time homemaker. It is frustrating to try to feel that I am a worthwhile person because I have chosen to be a full-time homemaker. However, it is difficult to find self-worth because there is not a paycheck. I still believe that being a full-time homemaker can be a very creative career.

HEAVY PROFESSIONAL DEMANDS

Many study participants are so busy that they have difficulty maintaining mentor and other relationships once considered meaningful and precious. This is described by two study participants in the following statements:

My most important mentor was the owner of a gymnastics school that I attended. He was also an M.D. He continually challenged me to expand, to use my mind and body. I discontinued my relationship when the demands of my medical school curriculum increased so much that there was no time for it. I love and respect him and I now try to challenge others to use their resources.

* *

There aren't enough hours in the day and I run out of energy. I am often undecided about what I really like or would like to be doing because so much time is spent on making do with the best of a situation... My husband stays at home, takes care of our child and does his art work. I am torn between traditional female upbringing and feminist anger and drive. I am particularly upset today because I have just turned 29 and I am successful only in business. My creative interests have been pushed aside.

UNSUCCESSFUL EXPERIENCES WITH MENTORS

Unsuccessful experiences with mentors may spell the doom of the relationship. Several varieties of unsuccessful experiences will be illustrated with responses from study participants. In the first, the relationship was ended when the mentor fired the mentee:

She was supportive of me and taught me a lot about the field. Our relationship ended with my termination of the job. She fired me. I feel she's a wonderful person who acted as she had to under the circumstances, being true to her own self.

In the next statement, a young woman describes her distress in a relationship characterized by hurt feelings and a sense of oppression:

I have had several minor mentors and I am still looking for a dance mentor. My earliest mentor taught me dance. She had a sense of no limits to what's possible to accomplish. She was a model of a strong woman. I quit working with her in distress about the way she treated me and how I took it out on myself. My greatest frustration is living in an oppressive society which systematically mistreats and encourages mistreatment of most people in society...

The following statement came from a young man who seems to have had several unsuccessful mentor relationships and a pattern of job and career instability.

Oh, Epicurus would have been a good mentor for me. Unfortunately his 200 treatises have been lost. What a relief!

My relationship with my most important mentor ended when we had nothing to say to one another. While I was manufacturing my phrases I felt that the earth was falling through space and I was falling with it at a speed that made me dizzy.

CREATING AN UNCONVENTIONAL CAREER

Many creative young people find they have to develop their own jobs/careers. Strangely, the creation of an unconventional career seems to doom mentor relationships. It may have been, however, that these mentor relationships had limited depth and caring:

> My current job was designed and implemented by myself and took much effort. Since this job had not existed before, there was no one to help. My mentor seemed irrelevant and was not at all in tune with anything so unconventional . . .My wife and I have taken part-time work so that we could raise our children together. In the next five years our children will be in the later years of elementary school and we hope to develop career options at that time.

Another illustration came from a young woman who is developing an unconventional career as a naturopath in a spiritually-oriented community. She considers her parents as her mentors during her early years and a woman 53 years her senior as her most important mentor. Although she still lives under their influence, she considers that developing an unconventional career somewhat alienates them from her and that she and her husband must create their careers with little help from mentors:

> I feel that the road I am taking now, though it may not seem creative in a conventional performance oriented sense, is a very creative act. We are learning through psychology, physiology and anatomy to help people make creative, positive changes in their lives. On my own, I am drawing, singing and doing work with my dreams. They are all activities that mirror to me my own creative impulse—to create, to feel joy. I have come from a creative family in which my parents were both performers. The most honored gift they gave me was the notion that humans need to create, to feel joy . . .

CHAPTER SIX

Careers Without Mentors

The preceding three chapters dealt with responses from the 46% of the longitudinal study participants with mentors. This chapter searches for wisdom in responses from the 54% who claimed not to have a mentor. The most important material from their data involves efforts to understand why they did not claim mentors and what the possible consequences were. It must be acknowledged that the data does not supply "proof" either of causal or consequential relationships. However, I have drawn upon my long years of professional experience in trying to understand such matters, what is known from other sources, and my own powers of logic and reason in trying to see possible connections between follow-up responses and not having a mentor.

POSSIBLE REASONS FOR NO MENTOR

• Rejection of Achievement Expectations of Society

From many responses by study participants, it is clear that they "walked away from the achievement expectations of society," and have deliberately chosen to live low-key lives. Sometimes this decision was clearcut and without conflict. With others, the decision has been made with ambivalence and consequent struggle, inconsistency of behavior and a tinge of indecisiveness.

To attain a low-key, relaxed lifestyle, some participants withdrew from the metropolitan, fast-paced environment they grew up in and moved to rural areas where social expectations are different. The following statement came from a young man who made such a move before completing his undergraduate work:

> My main directions are to my family and friends. We live in what one might describe as an alternative lifestyle. My relationships within my family and with friends are more open and less aggressive or self-oriented than almost anyone I know. We do not live in any kind of drug culture or commune but relate to the culture around us on their terms to the necessary extent.

Some participants deliberately chose jobs in which they might live lives with as few "hassles" as possible. This statement was made by a highly creative young man who is a janitor and is now classified as a maintenance supervisor:

My goal is to live my life with as few hassles as possible. I have long had a love for repairing and putting together bicycles. I have won some prizes in competitions for custom-built bicycles. I rebuild motorcycles, restore and refinish antiques, do woodwork, collect comics and work with scale models.

I am still involved in too many hassles. Being a working class hero is kind of a frustration itself. But watching this world tear itself apart with all of these power struggles going on and nothing being accomplished by them except more fighting is my biggest frustration. I would like to be someone that could put a stop to where this world is going.

Some participants are still interested in learning through original research and discovery. However, they want to do this in a relaxed, low-pressure context they can control without dependence on grants, consultants or even mentors. As one young man, a research biologist in the wildlife management field, put it:

I have no very serious frustrations. I do not think I have enough free time to really develop substantial, satisfying outside interests, but my job is so closely tied to my recreational interests that it doesn't really affect me.

I would like to own my own fairly large chunk of wild land on which I could both enjoy my leisure time with ease and conduct field research on various topics of interest to me.

Many who have chosen this lifestyle seem happy with it and their greatest dream is to continue. This is illustrated by a young man who builds transformers for farmers' electric fences:

I want to continue doing what I am doing now. It would be good to be a little richer, but this does not matter much.

A few who chose the low-key life admit to occasional moments of doubt and regret about making such a choice. Such was exemplified by a creative young man:

I had planned on going to the University of Minnesota after two years at Metro, but I couldn't make up my mind. I am sorry I dropped out and may go back after age 30 and become an engineer. I am a research technician with_____

_____ . I do plan to make a career change. I think more responsibility will be good for me and I'll be less likely to become bound with my job. Also I'll make more money.

I love green house plants and I grow pot indoors. I enjoy being by myself but I like to work with people. I have never been married but I am in a close relationship now and I am working toward marriage, but it will be hard to give up my independence in marriage.

In my current lifestyle I am at home three nights a week and during that time I enjoy smoking pot. I don't smoke much with other people but it is something that I really enjoy by myself . . .

For my future dream, I would choose a low key, mellow life, be an engineer making $30,000 a year, happily married with one child, owning a duplex and living in half of it. There would be money for a vacation and more time to spend with friends.

In all of these statements I sense a desire to maintain control over one's life. One might speculate that having a mentor would be too great a threat to this control.

● Fear of Rejection

Some participants said they had been raised in highly competitive, discouraging and high-achieving families in which they had felt rejected. One young woman described some of her struggles with this problem:

My family's lack of support of my field of interest has been frustrating . . . My family is very competitive and male-oriented. I grew up thinking I was the least of the bunch and that was tough on my self-esteem. I did not develop social skills. By the time I graduated from high school, my self-confidence was minimal . . . I became psychotic . . . I brought myself back to reality by myself. I never told anyone what it was like for nearly 10 years . . . I have a greater empathy for young people growing up in competitive, discouraging, high-achieving families.

Another young woman put it this way:

My greatest frustration is having self-imposed limitations that I've created myself. I am gradually coming to terms with these. I have let fear of rejection and failure inhibit me from letting people in on how I'm feeling and consequently have felt resentful and frustrated.

• Feelings of Isolation and Loneliness

Some participants apparently have been unable to seek or accept a mentor relationship because of their feeling of isolation and loneliness. Such a situation is described by a highly intelligent, below average creative young woman:

> I have never had a mentor. I'm not good at being under people's wings. I've had a couple of great psychotherapists but that's not the same thing. I spent my high school years pretty depressed. My father died suddenly when I was 14 . . . I'm single. My relationships with men have been poor generally and non-existent recently . . . For a long time (late elementary school into college), I was pretty isolated. A lot of my emotion and creativity was invested in writing poetry . . .

• Rebelliousness

While turning away from people may have interfered with the establishment of a mentor relationship for some participants, turning against adults in their environment may have prevented development of such a relationship among others. Yet if they had had a mentor, the rebelliousness might have been averted. One young woman illustrated this aspect of the problem:

> During my last two years of high school, I entered a tumultuous period of my life. Unfortunately, I did not have a mentor or revered adult to guide me. I went through a period of rebellion in which I abandoned everything I had been pushed toward (recognition, academic achievement, financial success, etc.). Instead I chose a course with no goals—a day-to-day existence. I was extremely lost and lonely. I am fortunate that I was not the victim of some disastrous occurrence because my own behavior did not protect me. Eventually I pulled together enough self-esteem to pursue a direction independent of my parents or a male companion.

One highly creative young man who never had a mentor chose the life of a revolutionary. In the following excerpts he tells part of his story:

> I dropped out of school to get a factory job and do rev-

olutionary organizing and agitation among the working class. I was a tool and die apprentice for two years and this has helped me get a job.

I want to contribute to the movement that will overthrow the system where a handful of super rich bloodsuckers run society, exploiting those who produce everything, oppressing women and minorities, and running our society . . .

My dream is to be able to do whatever will enable me to make the greatest contribution to advancing society from this dog-eat-dog system, to one which all humanity voluntarily and consciously transforms itself and the world.

Don't you think there are some of us out here, influenced by the tremendous upheavals of the '60s, the antiwar movement, the Black Liberation struggle, the cultural revolution in China, who have more on our minds than a career, a bunch of awards, a wife, two kids, a house in the suburbs, a station wagon and a color TV?!

• Independent Spirit, Driving Curiosity

Several participants described an independent spirit and/or a driving sense of curiosity and inquisitiveness that may have made establishment of a mentor relationship difficult. A creative young man seems to reflect this independent spirit:

I dropped out of college. There was nothing I wanted to gain from school, so it was a waste of my time to continue. I felt that what I wished to learn I could do on my own. Twice I took time off to travel around Europe with my wife for periods of six months each time. I established a good business and I have been able to help a good many people better their lives. I want to be an influential factor in making some people's lives better. Through my own business I am able to help a lot of people find some financial security and emotional freedom.

Another describes a driving sense of curiosity and inquisitiveness that may have worked against his establishment of a mentor relationship:

The greatest spur to achievement is my driving sense of curiosity and inquisitiveness. My greatest obstacle is my aversion to structured environments for education and careers.

> My biggest frustration is finding time to do all of the things I want to do and to see all I want to see, and go to all of the places I haven't visited in the limited time that I have.

● **Religious Fervor**

In a few cases, religious fervor and commitment may have interfered with the establishment of mentor relationships. Faith is placed in guidance from a higher power making the guiding, protecting hand of a human mentor inconsequential. This attitude is reflected in the following statement by a young woman:

> Since I have a family, I feel my main goal is to raise my children to be responsible and loving and following the Lord Jesus. Otherwise, I would consider a different career, maybe medicine or opening a craft shop or boutique.
>
> I feel that the most important commitment in my life is to my Lord and Saviour Jesus Christ and raising my children accordingly. It is harder than I thought it would be and takes much more time and planning.

● **Poverty**

Poverty may have been an important factor in the failure of several participants to find mentors. Since their schools had no mentor programs and their families lacked professional or business connections, this may be a reasonable speculation. Poverty seems to have been a deterrent to the development of healthy self-concepts in each case, compounding the problem of finding mentors. These comments come from a woman with creativity and intelligence test scores in the upper one percent of national norms in first grade and below average creativity scores and only slightly above average intelligence test scores three years later:

> I dropped out of school when I was in the tenth grade to take care of the younger members of my family. In a way I regret dropping out but it was the only thing I could do then. I would like to go back to school some time and finish high school so I can take nurse training, something I am really interested in. I probably won't do it as I am not very smart.

A similar story is told by a young man who lived in a government housing project near his elementary school. When he was in third grade his creativity score also placed him in the upper one percent of national norms. Later, while his creativity diminished, he managed to complete high school and spent four years in the Air Force. After this, he entered college but had to work to support himself and had not quite completed his undergraduate degree at the time of the followup. He wrote:

> Upon completing my degree I hope to get a job as a broker. Getting my degree has taken me a long time, about seven years already. I am still single and I cannot yet support a wife. I would like to grow spiritually the rest of my life.

A third participant handicapped by poverty had the advantage of a family which expected him to educate himself and attain success. In his words:

> My greatest frustration has been economic limitations during my school years and even now, and the question of getting a job after passing the Bar examinations. I am handicapped by not knowing any older lawyers and not having family connections in the law field. I am discouraged by this and the significant glut of lawyers on the market but I still dream of being a successful lawyer mixed later with a position as a state representative or senator.

● Career Indecision and Unconventional Career Aspirations

Career indecision and the choice of unconventional career goals seem to be important mentor-finding deterrents. In the case of career indecision, the youth generally had no real passion for a particular field, making the establishment of a mentor relationship unlikely. Such a person usually doesn't know who might be an appropriate mentor. For people with unconventional career aspirations, no appropriate mentor may be available to provide guidance. Study participants who experienced career indecision wrote:

> I am still having trouble deciding what career to be associated with that I can achieve success in. I am now an insurance agent but I think I would like to own and operate my own restaurant.

One creative young woman with many interests and no focus said:

> I am now director and administrator of a child-care community. I enjoy the work and like the self-employment. I would like to begin a part-time career in free-lance photography

which is currently a hobby. I am also thinking about work as a counselor. Also I would like to design clothing for mastectomy patients and publish a book on my life at some appropriate time, something to make life less frustrating for cancer patients . . .

Another participant gave this picture of diverse, unfocused interests and talents:

I started to go to college but lost interest, became bored and saw no purpose. I plan to return to school after over 10 years, possibly to be an LPN (Licensed Practical Nurse). I have worked as a teacher aide, factory worker, park attendant and headstart assistant. I traveled to Mexico, Africa and all over the USA and worked at many various jobs. I do some things in music (guitar), song writing, photography, herbal medicine, plant identification, etc.

One man still dreams of a career in outer space but is beginning to realize that may not become a reality for him.

I am a chip maker and caught up in the corporate life of high technology. I am not sure what keeps me going. It is very frustrating to see how slow all of the activities I am involved in are. It is also frustrating to know that I probably will never get into outer space or comprehend the universe about me. I would like to travel into outer space with members of a more advanced civilization. Perhaps I can take a year off from work and sail the oceans of the world.

SOME PROBLEMS OF CAREERS WITHOUT MENTORS

Participants without mentors seem to be characterized more frequently by certain problems than their peers with mentors. While it cannot be established with certainty that these problems are a consequence of not having a mentor, it seems clear that these problems are far more common among the mentorless than among those with mentors. I shall identify and illustrate the most frequently indicated problems and offer speculations about possible connections.

• Lack of Career Goal or Focus

The most frequently mentioned problem of the mentorless is the lack of career goals. It is not clear if this stems from not having a mentor or if the lack of a career goal or focus prevented the establishment of a mentor relationship. Consider the following comments by a highly creative woman:

> My greatest obstacle has been my inability to focus on a specific career goal that effectively makes use of my creative talents. I have difficulty in setting goals to be achieved in the future. I have not been able to come to a decision on motherhood. How does having a child affect my career?

One man described his lack of career focus as follows:

> It is hard for me to focus my energies. I uselessly scatter my time over too many projects. I lack the credentials to back my knowledge and insight at work, but I have been very inventive in creating computer programs to solve many business and management problems. I was married briefly and divorced but feel that the experience—of failing in a relationship—in many ways freed my own creative juices and my life.

Another young man said this about his lack of career goals:

> My biggest obstacle has been the lack of personal goals, ambition and aggressiveness. I went into the Marine Corps for two years because I had been driving a truck for a year and knew that I did not want to make a career of that. I also knew that I was not ready to go back to school. I have had and continue to have a hard time deciding what I want to do with my life—what I want to be when I grow up . . . I think this results not from a lack of interests but from having too many interests and desires.

Another male described his career wanderings as follows:

> I was admitted to the Honors Program but I still dropped out. I have had a variety of jobs: driver, phone counselor, laboratory technician, carpenter's apprentice, clothing importer, furniture moving business, etc. I am now a part of a group that collectively owns and manages a bicycle shop. I order the bikes as well as do repair, sales, teaching, etc. I am planning to change careers, however, probably management. I also keep very busy with a big variety of creative hobbies.

Still another creative male describes his lack of career focus:

> I have a BS in Environmental Design with additional training

in accounting. I have worked as an accountant but I am con-
sidering a change to computer science. I took time out for
two years to build a couple of companies. I feel frustrated
that I lack accomplishment due to lack of ambition, aggres-
siveness and discipline.

**

My dreams include: becoming an architect, a computer prog-
rammer, an accountant—taking control of my life—designing
and arranging my own environment and moving away from
society. Actually I am happy with myself. I feel that I am one
of the most creative people I know personally. I do not tend
to do things in, or care for socially acceptable activities.

• Lack of Enthusiasm or Love for Anything

While some participants have too many enthusiasms and a consequent lack of focus, others find nothing to be enthusiastic about or
"fall in love with." The following are illustrative statements by some
participants:

I have done nothing for a long period of time that I found
meaningful—either in work, community or personal/family.
Presently I am very busy in school and work, which frustrates
my growing involvement in the community and personal/
family interactions. I have lacked the personal self-discipline
for continued efforts in one line of endeavor. I cannot find
the time or energy for creative activities in face of the demands of work and related learning.

**

My current lifestyle is very hedonistic and work is something
to be avoided and minimized. I work to make a living and
most of the energy spent in law school is not spent with any
enthusiasm. I feel it is a lack of strong values, goals or be-
liefs which would act as a light at the end of the tunnel,
making an effort toward that light meaningful.

• Missed Opportunities

Some participants feel that not having a mentor caused them to miss
beneficial career opportunities. Two statements illustrate this problem:

My biggest frustration is not getting the opportunities that

I'd like to have in order to do what I know I can do. I dream of owning my own business . . .

* *

I would like to be a social worker or probation officer. I have been working two jobs for almost a year, just to make ends meet. I would like to be able to quit both jobs and attend school until I get my degree.

● Fear of Pressures to Conform

Comments in the follow-up questionnaires from several participants indicate they avoided mentor relationships out of fear of pressure to conform with conventional lifestyles. This statement by a multi-talented young woman illustrates the problem:

> I still feel hostile towards conventional lifestyles—marriage, family-rearing, house-buying, etc. I feel I've been put under pressure to conform from all sides and have been ridiculed and outcast because I haven't conformed in personal or pro-fessional life. I get sharp criticism from both family and friends and must say this apparent lack of understanding and acceptance is damaging to my self-concept. I feel like a retarded adolescent who hasn't matured according to plan, society's plan . . . When I'm inspired I can surprise people with my promptness, dedication to a goal, quickness and readiness to contribute all I have.

● Frustrated Creativity

Although frustrated creativity is not unique to mentorless participants, its occurrence was far more frequent among them. This is to be expected since there is a statistically significant correlation between both creative achievement and creative lifestyle measures and whether a person has a mentor or not. The following examples are from mentorless study participants:

> I am frustrated by my job and I am looking for another. I want something with more creative involvement. I am very frustrated creatively. My dream would be to find a passion for something in my life, i.e., career fulfillment, a marriage in which this frustration about creativity has been worked through, be a publisher, an advertising account executive or weaver.

I feel that I should have accomplished more by this time. Recently my creative output has been unsatisfactory. My frustration with people and situations sometimes causes me to explode in irrational anger and a form of violence I never thought was inside me. This anger appears misdirected and is hurtful to the people I love.

My dream for my life ten years hence is to have found a much larger audience for my plays. I would also like to expand my own potential to include the publication of short stories and novels.

* *

I am still looking for a mentor. I think my greatest obstacle is my insecurity and anxiety. My hidden desire is to become involved in urban planning. I am spurred by my desire to succeed and to be as independent as possible in my work. I want to pursue and experience new challenges and find out what I am capable of doing. I think my creativity is frustrated because I want to do well at things and never know for sure that I have.

● Non-creative Jobs that Drain Creative Energy

Many participants, including those with mentors, have jobs offering few creative outlets. However, they succeed in finding energizing creative activities outside the workplace. Some even regard activities outside their employment as their real careers—their "work" or "calling." However, the mentorless more frequently report that their jobs "for pay" drain their creative energies—something they find debilitating. A few statements from questionnaire responses are illustrative:

My greatest spur is my love for music and the enjoyment I have in performing and in composing. My greatest obstacle is having to work at an uncreative job to pay the bills and this drains my creative energy. I get tired of fending for myself all the time in order to support my music habits. My work wears me out so I have little energy to do much else . . .

* *

I wish that I could spend less time making money and could spend more money on the things I love. Of course, it would be nice to be able to earn my living doing something I love.

** **

I completed two years of college in speech pathology but I am now an apprentice pipefitter. No one has ever encouraged my creativity, although I was editor of the school paper in high school and was an officer in student government.

I apologize for never mailing your previous questionnaire. I started to fill it out and became rather depressed. Now that I have completed this one, I really feel depressed. I guess I never realized how frustrated my creativity has been.

(NOTE: This participant's measured IQ was reported to be 140 by one test and 133 by another. Scores on the *Torrance Test of Creativity* placed her in the creatively gifted group.)

Some highly creative young people deliberately seek jobs making few demands upon them and which will leave them energy for creativity. A highly creative, mentorless contemporary of subjects in this study, has written me on several occasions about his struggle to maintain creativity and gain acceptance of some of his unquestionably brilliant ideas. In the following statement, he reports his good luck in obtaining a job of this type:

Fortunately, I have at last the dream job of every genius— civil service nightwatchman! I was having a cup of tea while at "work" and all of a sudden the Muse tapped me on the shoulder and said, "Hey, dummy, this is how to do the **Last Supper** in a new way." I quickly drew the vision before it vanished.

Whenever this happens it is as though I were under the higher force. And I had no intention at all of doing a **Last Supper**! The only hint is that the day before I perused a reproduction of Rubens' **Last Supper** at the library and remarked about the good humor it showed. Also until then I had not known that Rubens had done a **Last Supper**, but then I turned the page and gave it no further thought, at least on the conscious level . . . If I had to think of these things myself, I would not have been able to.

Such creative events, however, are not likely to occur on the "paid" job unless there is time for incubation. With a mentor who could help him learn how "to play the game," this young man might become recognized as the "genius" he calls himself.

Some study subjects also had noncreative jobs that did not drain all of their creative energies. They performed these noncreative jobs with competence and calmness and channeled their creative energies and abilities into activities outside the workplace. A moderately-creative young woman explained:

> I haven't channeled my creative ability into my career. The field I chose is one of the most traditionally dull and boring fields (accounting). I do derive some pleasure from it, however, but I have compensated by using my spare time for my artistic talents. I draw, using my spare time for my artistic talents. I draw, paint, work in stained glass, sew, design. My husband and I have transformed an old brick period dump into a semimodern home at a considerable saving compared to new homes . . .

• Emotional Problems, Alcoholism, Drug Abuse

While none of the high creative individuals with mentors reported any emotional breakdowns, alcoholism or drug addiction, several of their mentorless counterparts reported such problems. Two of the mentorless could not complete the second questionnaire because they were under psychiatric care.

These statements were written by a mentorless highly creative young woman whose creativity was diminished by emotional problems:

> I have had an incredible struggle in my life with emotional problems that have manifested themselves in food and body obsessions. I have had a lot of therapy. It has been about a year since I have been able to deal with these symptoms and underlying problems with success. I belong to a group called "Over-eaters Anonymous" which is a step program like AA . . . I am very concerned about what it means to be a woman and an artist. I am very concerned about my relationship with my lover. I am very concerned about nuclear energy.

The following was offered by a highly creative male about the ravages of alcoholism:

> I am a recovering alcoholic who has lost the years between 20 and 30. An additional year was spent in Vietnam. Recovery is slow but things are getting better. Anything is better

than my former lifestyle was. It was simply a halt in emotional, spiritual and social development. After marking time, I'm finally progressing again: towards what I wish I knew.

My dream for ten years from now is to be self-employed in a professional role rendering useful assistance to others.

My greatest spur is remaining sober, which marks the difference between creative living and mere existence.

My greatest obstacle is my limited self-esteem.

My greatest frustration is having to make up for lost time. Having to go through an orderly progression to attain the goals I desire is frustrating.

These thoughts were reported by a mentorless participant involved in drug abuse and who is still struggling to clear his record so he can function as a professional:

I served an 18-month prison sentence for a narcotics violation. After high school, I moved to _____ and skied for one season and did not enter college until about a year ago. I have worked as a janitor, cabinet maker and data analyst. I have won several local sailboat regattas and have held exhibitions of my photography. I would like to be a behavioral management consultant in the health care field. In two or three years I shall return to Federal court for expungment of all charges against me and the sealing of public records. This could seriously affect my ability to maintain professional status with a publicly accessible Federal record.

CHAPTER SEVEN

What Might Be Done To Improve Mentoring?

The longitudinal study on which this publication is based draws upon the experiences of 220 young adults (about 30 years old) who grew up mostly in middle class Minnesota families between 1950 and 1980 and attained relatively high levels of education. The data raises some important questions about the mentor relationship as presently conceived in schools, colleges, business and industry. I shall try to identify some of them as well as action that seems appropriate.

First, the study findings question the assumption that the mentor relationship is a brief, transitory one with a definite cutoff date. Sometimes mentor relationships are short and transitory, with a termination date. However, 52% of the mentor relationships reported by study participants persisted at the time of the follow-up. The average length of the mentor relationship was almost five years. It appears that those who establish mentoring programs in schools, colleges, businesses and elsewhere should recognize that the relationships are open-ended, creative and may be terminated at any time or might endure for a lifetime, undergoing whatever transformations may occur in the creative process.

In a creative mentor-mentee relationship, neither party knows where the process might go. There should be a willingness to let one thing lead to another, without fear that it will lead to anything damaging to either party. The relationship should be entered into with trust and there should be an awareness that while it might endure for a lifetime, it must change with time and the mentor must continue to grow. There must also be an awareness that the mentee may grow in ways making the relationship no longer useful. Even when this point is reached, the spiritual aspects of the relationship may endure though the mentor and mentee may never see one another. In fact, if the relationship is a deep and caring one, this is quite likely to occur.

Both the mentor and mentee should recognize that the power of the mentor is limited and that the power of the relationship may be limited. Though the mentor may have prestige and power, he/she may not have enough to insure that the mentee has the opportunities that he/she desires. Though there may be a certain "magic" in the relationship and in the interventions of the mentor on behalf of the mentee, organizers of mentoring programs should guard against leading young people to expect too much from the relationship. For example, in organizing a mentoring program for freshmen in the fall of 1983, one university advertised the plan as "it's MAGIC." Freshmen were told that their university mentor can provide them assistance with: discussing your academic program, setting career goals, improving interpersonal relationships, enhancing use of leisure time, developing leadership abilities, increasing cultural awareness and appreciation, solving personal and financial problems, identifying and locating experiences of interest and getting involved with campus clubs and activities.

The only obligations specified for freshmen were:

- Meet your mentor in informal settings throughout the year.
- Participate in an assessment project to assist us in designing a MAGIC program especially for you.

Such advertising could lead freshmen to have unreasonable expectations and fail to assume responsibility for solving their problems and taking charge of their lives.

Those who organize and foster mentor programs also should recognize that the mentor relationship may in time become one of friendship, teacher, competitor, lover or father figure. If the relationship is a deep and caring one (and this seems to be a major characteristic of a genuine mentor relationship), any of these relationships may evolve. However, because of the caring nature, the outcomes are not likely to be harmful. However, this may be a necessary risk.

There is also a need for mentoring program organizers, as well as mentors and mentees, to be aware of the common obstacles to continuing, enduring mentor relationships. These include the frequently intimidating nature of some mentor relationships, setting too fast a pace and not respecting the natural pace of the mentee, making sacrifices to personal integrity, sex role barriers, racial barriers, behavior disapproved by the mentor, a philosophy of life incompatible with the acceptance of a mentor relationship, aversion to the institution or social system to which the mentor belongs, feelings of threat to the status quo ignited by the mentee and feelings of hurt, mistreatment or rejection.

Attention should be directed to the possible use of mentors for young children, especially creatively-gifted ones from disadvantaged families. Without such attention, these children are likely to sacrifice their giftedness by the time they emerge from the primary grades.

Schools as well as businesses and industries need to expand the pool from which they recruit mentors. While there is a need for mentors with a future orientation, there is also a need to have them with an historical orientation. Young people with a future orientation may lack some of the power and prestige of the usual pool of mentors. However, mentors influence the images of the future of their mentees and it would be foolhardy not to recognize and develop this aspect of mentoring. Retired people in business and industry, grandparents and other retired people in schools and families provide another pool of possible mentors. Virginia Ehrlich (1983) called attention to the potential of grandparents as mentors of young children. She urged parents to use the specialized knowledge of grandparents. She also maintains that grandparents will exert enormous energy locating special information to share with children.

Finally, there are some indications in the longitudinal study that a new and potentially important role may be emerging for mentors. A considerable number of participants attained their expertise through self-directed learning and/or a kind of apprenticeship with the assistance of a mentor. Since this expertise was not attained through a college or other accredited agency, there exists a new set of problems related to the validation of the expertise. In some cases, mentors have been able to certify the expertise of mentees through personal contacts or recommendations. This may become an increasing trend as change accelerates and as the attainment of professional expertise increasingly occurs through self-directed and experiential learning. Plowman (1979) has foreseen such a possibility and suggests that in the future socially approved mentors will determine that certain competencies have been mastered and certify that this has been done.

THE MOST IMPORTANT THINGS MENTORS CAN DO

I have done much thinking about the meaning of the findings reported in this volume. When the follow-up data was collected, I had known many of the study participants for 22 years. I still have contacts with many of them and even with some of their parents. On the basis of what I know about them and their accomplishments, as well as the things that have happened to them, I have tried to formulate a set of guidelines about the most important things mentors can do for gifted youth, especially the creatively gifted ones. These guidelines follow:

HELP THEM TO:

1. Be unafraid of "falling in love with something" and pursue it with intensity and in-depth. A person is motivated

most to do the things they love and can do best.

2. Know, understand, take pride in, practice, use, exploit and enjoy their greatest strengths.

3. Learn to free themselves from the expectations of others and to walk away from the games that others try to impose upon them.

4. Free themselves to play their own game in such a way as to make the best use of their strengths and follow their dreams.

5. Find some great teachers and attach themselves to these teachers.

6. Avoid wasting a lot of expensive, unproductive energy in trying to be well-rounded.

7. Learn the skills of interdependence and give freely of the infinity of their greatest strengths.

Post-High School Creative Achievement Questionnaire

Indicate whether you have achieved any of the following by underlining the appropriate words. On the line before any item you underline, indicate the number of times you have achieved it *since graduating from high school.*

____ Invented a patentable device.

____ Published an article in a scientific or professional journal.

____ Presented an original paper to a scientific or professional society.

____ Received a prize or award for a scientific or professional paper or project.

____ Published a poem, short story, feature story, or book.

____ Received a literary award or prize for creative writing or other journalism.

____ Edited a professional or literary paper or magazine.

____ Wrote or directed a play or choreographed a dance that was given at least one public performance.

____ Performed the lead role in a play, motion picture, TV production, or dance.

____ Received an award or prize for original work in drama or dance.

____ Received an award or prize for performance in drama or dance.

____ Composed music which was given at least one public performance.

____ Published original music composition.

____ Performed with or organized a professional musical group.

____ Received an award for a musical composition.

____ Received an award or prize for musical performance.

____ Held an exhibition of paintings, sculpture, photographs, etc.

____ Published art work (cartoon, photograph, illustrations) in a newspaper, magazine, or book.

_____ Received prize or award for work in art.

_____ Created advertising ideas that were implemented.

_____ Created original educational materials that were used by a wide audience.

_____ Won election to public office.

_____ Organized a political campaign.

_____ Organized own business, service, or professional organization.

_____ Received an award or special recognition for leadership of any kind.

_____ Conducted in-service education or training for co-workers.

_____ Conducted in-service education or training for workers in a different organization.

_____ Suggested modifications of existing practices or policies that were adopted by superiors or co-workers.

List below any creative achievements that are not covered by the above list.

_____

_____

_____

_____

Describe below what you consider your three most creative achievements since high school graduation. These may be in any area of life.

_____

_____

_____

_____

_____

Briefly describe the duties you perform in your present position.

_____

_____

_____

_____

What are your career ambitions, e.g., what position, responsibility, or rewards do you want to attain? What do you hope to accomplish?

_____

_____

_____

_____

_____

If you could do or be whatever you choose in the next 10 years, what would it be?

_____

_____

_____

_____

_____

_____

_____

_____

_____

_____

Creative Style Of Life
Achievement Questionnaire

Please describe an incident which occurred during the past month and which you think illustrates best the creativity that you display in your day to day life. It may be something that happened in your business or professional life, in your home, in your community—anywhere.

Within the past five years, have you (check as many as apply):

____ Organized an action-oriented group (e.g., an environmental group, community service group, advocacy group, nursery cooperative, food cooperative, etc.).

____ Designed and taught a new course.

____ Designed a house.

____ Designed a garden.

____ Been instrumental in starting a new educational venture (e.g., a preschool, special tutoring program, free school, program for the elderly, cancer or stroke group, etc.).

____ Participated in a group experience designed to foster personal change (e.g., encounter group, T-group, consciousness-raising group, Outward Bound, etc.).

____ Planned and led such a group.

____ Joined a new religion.

____ Had a striking religious experience.

____ Taken up meditation.

_____ Completed a poem, story, novel, or article that has not been published.

_____ Completed a musical composition that was not performed publicly.

_____ Choreographed a dance that was not publicly performed.

_____ Completed a painting or other art work that was not publicly exhibited.

_____ Made original designs for clothing.

_____ Planned and carried out an unorthodox journey (e.g., bicycling through Gobi Desert, transcontinental camel ride, rowing to Alaska, etc.).

_____ Been instrumental in bringing about a significant change in rules or operating procedures in an organization.

_____ Worked out a new way of doing an everyday task (e.g., housework, getting to work, routine office matters, etc.).

_____ Learned a new skill.

_____ Become seriously involved in a new sport.

_____ Become seriously involved in a new hobby.

Note below any creative activities in your private life that are not covered in the above list:

_____

_____

_____

How much creativity or ingenuity do you think you bring to such household tasks as cooking, shopping, child care, entertaining, gardening, car maintenance and repair, decorating, remodeling, etc.? Give one example.

_____

_____

_____

References

ATKINSON, C., ALBERTS, R., BELCHER, F., BELLMAN, G., GROTE, R., HAYES J. R., LAIRD, D., MAHONEY, F.X. & MIRABEL, T. E. Management development roles: coach, sponsor, and mentor. *Personnel Journal*, 1980, 59, 918-921.

BLACKBURN, R. T., CHAPMAN, D. W. & CAMERON, S. M. "Cloning" in academe: mentorship and academic careers. *Research in Higher Education*, 1981, 15, 315-327.

BRIDGES, R. D. Mentors open new careers and hobby vistas for youth. *Phi Delta Kappan*, 1980, 62, 199.

COLLINS, E. G. C. & SCOTT, P. (eds.) Everyone who makes it has a mentor. *Harvard Business Review*, 1978, 56(4), 89-101.

COLSON, S. The evaluation of a community-based career education program for gifted and talented students as an administrative model for an alternative program. *Gifted Child Quarterly*, 1980, 24, 101-106.

COOK, M. F. Is the mentor relationship primarily a male experience. *Personnel Administrator*, 1979, 24(11), 82-86.

CRANDALL, H. B. Are mentors necessary for successful career? *Direct Marketing*, 1981, 44(6), 124-130.

EHRLICH, V. Grandparents and gifted grandchildren. *Gifted Children Newsletter*, August 1983, 4(8), 1-3, 13.

FEVERS, S. & DIAMOND, H. Husband as mentor; "you can do it": an interview with Stelle Fevers. *Educational Horizons*, 1978, 57(2), 90-96.

FITT, L. W. & NEWTON, D. A. When the mentor is a man and the protege a woman. *Harvard Business Review*, 1981, 59(2), 56, 58, 60.

GOERTZEL, M. G., GOERTZEL, V. & GOERTZEL, T. G. *300 eminent personalities*. San Francisco: Jossey-Bass, 1978.

GOERTZEL, V. & GOERTZEL, M. G. *Cradles of eminence*. Boston: Little, Brown, 1962.

HALCOMB, R. Mentors and the successful woman. *Across the Board*, 1980, 17(2), 13-18.

KAUFMANN, F. A. A follow-up study of the 1964-68 Presidential Scholars. (Doctoral dissertation, University of Georgia, 1979). *Dissertation Abstracts International*, 1980, 40, 5794-A.

KELLEY, L. On the job. *Working Woman*, 1982 (May).

LEVINSON, D. J. *The seasons of man's life*. NYC: Knopf, 1978.

MANSERGH, G. G., JESKA-SILRUM, L., AMES, D. & HANSEN, M. *1982 summer mentorship program*. Minneapolis, MN: The Educational Cooperative Service Unit of the Metropolitan Twin Cities Area, 1982.

MORSBACH, H. Socio-psychological aspects of persistence in Japan. *Japan Times*, 1978 (December 20), 7-8.

NOLLER, R. B. *Mentoring: a voiced scarf*. Buffalo, NY: Bearly Limited, 1982.

NOLLER, R. B. & FREY, B. R. *Mentoring: an annotated bibliography.* Buffalo, NY: Bearly Limited, 1983.

PLOWMAN, P. D. Futuristic views of education: images of what might be. *Journal of Creative Behavior,* 1978, *12,* 90-97.

QUINN, B. C. The influence of same-sex and cross-sex mentors on the professional development and personality characteristics of women in human services. *Dissertation Abstracts International,* 1980, *41,* 1498-1499-A.

ROE, A. *The making of a scientist.* NYC: Dodd, Mead, 1953.

ROWE, M. P. Building mentorship frameworks as part of an effective equal opportunity ecology. In Farley, J. (ed.), *Sex discrimination in higher education.* Ithaca, NY: Cornell University Press, 1981.

TORRANCE, E. P. *Guiding creative talent.* Englewood Cliffs, NJ: Prentice-Hall, 1962. (Reprinted by William Krieger Publishers, P. O. Box 9542, Melbourne, FL 32901)

TORRANCE, E. P. *Rewarding creative behavior.* Englewood Cliffs, NJ: Prentice-Hall, 1965.

TORRANCE, E. P. *The Torrance Tests of Creative Thinking: norms-technical manual.* Bensenville, IL: Scholastic Testing Service, 1974. (Originally published by Personnel Press in 1966)

TORRANCE, E. P. Growing up creatively gifted: a 22-year longitudinal study. *Creative Child and Adult Quarterly,* 1980, *5,* 148-158, 170.

TORRANCE, E. P. Predicting the creativity of elementary school children (1958-1980)—and the teacher who "made a difference." *Gifted Child Quarterly,* 1981, *25,* 55-62.

TORRANCE, E. P. Role of mentors in creative achievement. *Creative Child and Adult Quarterly,* 1983, *8,* 8-15, 18.

TORRANCE, E. P. & WU, T. H. A comparative longitudinal study of adult creative achievements of elementary school children identified as highly intelligent and as highly creative. *Creative Child and Adult Quarterly,* 1981, *6,* 71-76.

TOYNBEE, A. Is America neglecting her creative minority? In Taylor, C. W. (ed.), *Widening horizons in creativity.* NYC: John Wiley, 1964.

Women finally get mentors of their own. *Business Week,* 1978 (October 23), 74, 79-80.